THE DEMOCRATIC CHALLENGE

Series Editor: MEIC STEPHENS

The Democratic Challenge

John Osmond

GOMER

First Impression — 1992

ISBN 0 86383 927 4

Printed in Wales by
J. D. Lewis and Sons Ltd., Gomer Press, Llandysul, Dyfed

Whatever the peoples of Wales are, they are not a homogeneous group. Many of them don't know very much about one another for a start, and often lack familiarity with one another's territory. It is probably the case, for instance, that more people in the Valleys have visited Marbella than Machynlleth.

Traditionally, Welsh identity has been carried by a separate language, nonconformity in religion, and an economy dependent on extractive industries. Yet, in the last few generations these traditional vehicles of inheritance have all faltered in their tracks: the language has declined from being spoken by a majority of the population to around 20 per cent; Wales, like the rest of Britain, has become a secular rather than a religious society; and coal-mining and slate-quarrying have all but disappeared.

The lack of cohesion is further emphasized by the instability of the Welsh population. During the 1980s an estimated 40,000 to 50,000 people moved into Wales every year with a similar number moving out. This means that before the end of the century perhaps as much as a third of Wales's 3 million population will have moved within a twenty-year period.

This is a major demographic shift whose impact affects different communities disproportionately. Many rural villages in north and west Wales are seeing native young people displaced by a combination of older, retired people, and sometimes younger people moving in because they can more easily afford the housing. In the Valleys of south Wales the trend is for people to move or at least commute to the coast and further afield to find work.

Again, it is often asserted that Wales is split into at least three regions—north, middle, and south—with each having more in common with adjacent parts of England than with each other. Political analysis has tended to follow this 'three-Wales model', though adjusting the boundaries to take account of cultural cleavage. So we have Gwynedd, Ceredigion and Carmarthen—*Y Fro Gymraeg*, Plaid Cymru's stronghold; the Valleys, described as 'Welsh Wales' where Labour rules; and the contested remainder, sometimes referred to as 'British Wales', where Labour and occasionally Liberal Democrats fight the Conservatives.

Little wonder therefore that, taking all these elements together, questions about Welsh identity and the very image of the Welsh—what we are, and should or could be—constantly arise.

On the only occasion when the people of Wales had a clear opportunity to pronounce collectively on such questions, in the 1979 referendum, they appeared to reject emphatically an all-Wales political dimension. But was the four-to-one vote against a Welsh Assembly a self-conscious denial of any attempt to construct institutions on the identity of Wales as a whole? One interpretation, certainly, was that the result suggested that the political loyalty of the Welsh is first to Britain as a whole, and thereafter to local communities within Wales rather than to Wales itself.

Such an analysis, of course, assumes that all the Welsh took a broadly similar view. Yet, though the No vote registered fairly uniformly across Wales, it seemed to be motivated differently in different places. In the south-east, for instance, the accusation was made that the pro-Assembly lobby was dominated by a non-conformist, Welsh-speaking rural élite that wished to impose its values on the whole of Wales. In the north-west on the other hand, the fear was expressed that an Assembly would be dominated by equally alien, but socialist forces from the south.

That both perceptions were undoubtedly a caricature is not the point if that is what people felt. More obviously perhaps, the No vote reflected incredulity that 'another tier of government' was being proposed at the very time when the view was widespread that there was already too much government, too much bureaucracy, and at too great a cost.

Within the term bureaucracy in such arguments tend to be subsumed notions of democracy. It seems in the nature of the way people in Wales regard politics to confuse the two. Thus, even now politicians and journalists who ought to know better, refer to an Assembly as being another 'tier of government'.

What this ignores, of course, is that a sophisticated Welsh tier of government already exists, has done so certainly since 1964, and has consistently expanded. Some 80 per cent of public expenditure in Wales—around £6 billion annually—is now channelled through the Welsh Office and its related appointed bodies or quangos.

This bureaucratic tier of government was well in place at the time of the 1979 referendum. The trouble was that then it was run by the Labour Party. In 1979 the attitude of the large majority of Labour councillors, Labour place-people on the quangos (then a large majority), and most Labour MPs and constituency activists was quite simply, 'We're already running the show, why change?'

Thirteen years of Conservative control of the Welsh Office, together with the steady erosion of local government, has put a quite different complexion on that question. But mention of local government goes to the heart of the confusion between bureaucracy and democracy, a confusion that still persists. Few would deny, for instance, that over the past decade or so local government has been under attack. There has been a constant erosion of its financial autonomy while at the same time many of its functions have been chipped away or handed over wholesale to appointed bodies.

Yet this has aroused little response. Attitudes to local government in Wales, as probably in most other parts of the United Kingdom, are at best indifferent. There is very little appreciation of what local government does in providing some of our most basic life-support services. Rather, local councils are constantly attacked for wasting money. They are rarely defended, never loved, and usually blamed.

The attitude was typified by the director of the Wales CBI, Ian Kelsall, in an attack he made on a Welsh Assembly in the wake of the 1992 General Election:

> In my opinion I think we have councillors coming out of our ears and we cannot possibly sustain the argument that there is a lack of democracy in Wales. But what we do need is a rationalization of local government.[1]

What was meant by the last remark was a diminution of local government, a reduction in the number of authorities and, above all, a reduction in the number of councillors. It is instructive that all parties in Wales now share this view. A stark reality is that during

[1] *Western Mail,* 22 May 1992

the 1990s, if current trends continue unchecked, such autonomous local government as we have had in Wales—and, after all, this has been the only Welsh-based democratic government we have experienced—is likely to come to an end.

CITIZENS OR SUBJECTS?

An underlying problem is that we in Wales, in common with people in the rest of the United Kingdom with whom we share a very peculiar political culture, have a poorly developed democratic instinct. This is hardly surprising, since our constitution, such as it is, does not allow for citizenship. Constitutionally, we are not citizens in the United Kingdom, but subjects.

We are ruled by a Crown-centred Parliamentary oligarchy established more than four centuries ago in the bloodless non-revolution of 1688: a century before the people-centred revolutions in America and France heralded the industrial revolution. In that eighteenth and nineteenth-century great tide of history England/Britain was left, willingly, on the sidelines—indeed resisted and fought against it. It is one reason why Britain today is such a reluctant and difficult partner in the attempt to create institutions and political unity at the European level. Our culture of non-citizenship in Britain goes directly against the grain of the relatively mature sense of citizenship that is much more developed in most of the other European Community member-states. It's like mixing oil and water.

What happened in Britain four centuries ago was not a democratic revolution, but simply a fracturing of the unity of 'Crown in Parliament', and the reconstitution of the relationship with the emphasis placed upon Parliament rather than the Crown. To illustrate the point one only has to chronicle how, when the democratic principle was finally allowed during the nineteenth century, it was carefully and only gradually parcelled out, first to those who had an economic interest in the established state institutions, through their ownership of property. Thus the great 1832 Reform Act did not even hand the vote to the middle-class, but just 7 per cent of adult males who were freeholders and worth forty shillings a year. The proportion was gradually raised to

16 per cent in 1867, 28 per cent in 1884, and 74 per cent in 1918 when there was an abolition of the property qualification for men. It was in 1918, too, that women aged over thirty were allowed the vote for the first time. The principle of universal suffrage, one person one vote, aged eighteen and over and regardless of sex, was only finally established in 1948.

By this time, of course, the party system, reinforced by the Whips in the House of Commons, had effectively removed much of whatever power individual MPs may once have had. At the same time they retained a traditional proprietorial regard for their constituencies, reminiscent of their aristocratic forebears. Parliament was originally a squirearchy and this atmosphere persists. It is reflected, for instance, in the rejection by most MPs of proportional representation, and certainly any system that might weaken their personal identification with their constituencies, an identification which often amounts to a sense of ownership.

A problem with the English for the Welsh, who have to live so close to them, is that they are a very peculiar nationality. Most conventional nationalities the world over, and not least the Welsh, define their identity in terms of territory, language and a sense of the people as being the building-blocks of the nation. The English, however, have at best an ambiguous relationship with these characteristics. Who can draw a map of England? England is a country of the mind. It is either smaller than its actual territory, focused around an imagined 'Home Counties' rural arcadia, or larger: embracing the whole island of Britain (Northern Ireland is usually excluded) and formerly all those red bits on the map, still sometimes retained in the form of the Commonwealth. The English language is regionalized into dialects and accents on the one hand, while on the other, Americanized into a world alternative to Esperanto. But most significant of all, as already stated, there are no English *people*—only *subjects* under that Crown-Parliament hegemony established in 1688.

Understandably, the Welsh have difficulty in relating to this peculiar formation. To a large extent they share in it, especially where the monarchy is concerned. Indeed, the Welsh are often distinguishable from the English by their very enthusiasm for the Royal Family in all its forms. At the same time, however, the Welsh embrace self-consciously a sense of Britishness as being distinct from Englishness. This takes the form of a duality of identity, with Britishness seen as something different from both Welshness and Englishness.

The trouble is that where institutions are concerned, bound up as they are with notions of democracy and citizenship, Welshness is at odds with Britishness, which is why discussion of Welsh institutions is controversial, even subversive. Welsh institutions are inevitably connected to Welsh nationality, and in contrast to the neighbouring, peculiar English variety, Welsh nationality is inseparable from the people and democracy.

According to James Griffiths, the first Secretary of State for Wales, the creation of the Welsh Office in 1964 and the place in the British Cabinet it gave him, had come about as a result of a 'recognition of our nationhood'[2]. How far, however, was this recognition something that could be readily tied to conventional ideas of nationhood, built around institutions and a democratic culture? What James Griffiths was really referring to was a nationhood built on cultural distinguishing factors like language and religion, that in 1964 still predominated in the way Wales was imagined, both at home and abroad.

Looking back more than a decade to the pivotal experience of the 1979 referendum, one of the more interesting questions to ask is why the result in Wales and Scotland was so different. People tend to under-estimate the importance of the majority Yes vote in Scotland, partly because it did not reach the loaded 40 per cent of the electorate that Parliament required. The referenda in Wales and Scotland were held at exactly the same time and, in British terms, in exactly the same circumstances. That is to say, they were promoted by an unpopular Labour Government near the end of its term of office in the midst of an acute winter of discontent. To some extent the referendum was a plebiscite on that Government's record, at a time when government generally, because of economic failure, was unpopular.

Yet in Scotland in 1979 these pressures did not impact to anything like the same extent as in Wales. Arguably, the reason was

[2] Hansard: Welsh Grand Committee, First Sitting, 16 December 1964

because the Scots have retained a much stronger sense
ship, one much more people-centred than anywhere
United Kingdom, and one much more recognizable in
European terms. Ideas of Scottish citizenship rest relatively eas...
a society which, since 1707, has retained its own church and separate legal and education systems, not to mention the memory of the Parliament it had not so long ago. Arguably, too, this explains why, today, Scotland constitutes the leading potential edge for constitutional change in Britain.

The apparent Tory triumph in the 1992 General Election in Scotland was based on their confounding widespread expectations that they would lose at least half of their Scottish seats. In the event they increased their vote by just 1.6 to 25.7 per cent and held on to their eleven seats. Labour polled 39 per cent, Liberal Democrats 13 per cent and the SNP increased their vote from 14 to 21.5 per cent. What cannot be denied is that, led by John Major, the Tories chose to fight the 1992 Election in Scotland on their defence of an unchanged union, and emphatically lost.

There are indications that in the 1990s Wales is moving into a position much more like the Scottish than applied even less than thirty years ago, when the Welsh Office was first established. Though cultural markers, like language and religion, have lost some of the force they had then, others have arisen in their place. Overwhelmingly these have an institutional character, building on the Welsh Office itself—so much so that now it is possible to describe Welsh nationality as being propelled by a dynamic of institutions. These are developing as much in civil society as in the public arena, related to government and administration. There are now more than 500 organizations that operate at the all-Wales level and they multiply as each year passes.[3] But the most important, for the argument being pursued here, are based around the government machine itself, including local government, and in the field of broadcasting.

[3] A directory of Welsh 'associations, movements, bodies, committees and institutions', published by the Welsh Library Association in 1984, identified 466 organizations from Yr Academi Gymreig to the Young Women's Christian Association, which had Welsh offices and officials. There is no doubt the figure is rising. A good example is the twenty-seven listed groups now operating under the umbrella of *Y Fforwm Iaith* (the Welsh Language Forum).

Economically, too, with the demise of the nationalized industries in the 1980s—especially coal and much of steel—the Welsh economy has become less dependent on the British, moving closer to an evenly balanced profile. In the 1990s it is starting to make sense for the first time to talk in terms of planning for a Welsh economy. This is particularly the case when increasing European integration is making Brussels and Strasbourg a focus for government alongside London. Moreover, the European dimension, with its requirement that even the English have to address the issue of sovereignty, is also putting questions of citizenship very much on the agenda.

Identity and questions of nationality and democracy are closely bound up with these considerations, especially for the Welsh. But what can being a nation mean for Wales in the integrating Europe of the 1990s, when neighbouring England still retains its dominating cultural force? The Dutch writer, Herman Dooyeweerd, provides a useful starting-point:

> A nation is a people which has become conscious of its internal political solidarity.[4]

For Wales in the 1990s there can be no doubt that institutions carry the main weight of the required awareness and solidarity. So, in answer to the national question posed above: Wales consists of a people struggling to become a nation by progressively establishing their own institutions. It follows that democracy, how far it is understood, appreciated and applied, goes straight to the heart of the project.

THE DYNAMIC OF INSTITUTIONS

The second half of the twentieth century has been marked by an ambitious phase of institutional development in Wales. This has built on the foundation of the late Victorian and Edwardian era when first local government was established, closely followed by educational institutions like the University of Wales, the National

[4] Herman Dooyeweerd, 'A New Critique of Theoretical Thought' (Amsterdam, 1957), Part III, p. 470

Library, and the National Museum. This process was soc
by two world wars and the depression of the 1930s. Ho
the wake of World War II, as England gradually and painfu
coming to terms with being a medium-sized European
rather than a world imperial power, Wales was allowed more room for manoeuvre.

The critical moment came with the creation and then rapid development of the Welsh Office after 1964. Founded with just 225 civil servants, these grew to 1,210 inside ten years, and 2,300 by the early 1990s, with a further 1,500 in subordinate national institutions. During this period the Welsh Office saw its powers spread across virtually the whole of the domestic concerns of the Welsh people, starting with housing and local government, expanding to health and education and then to most aspects of the Welsh economy.

The budget of this emerging bureaucracy was very small at the start, just £48,000 in 1964. Within ten years, however, it had grown to £1.2 million. And by the 1991-2 financial year a very nearly mature network of developed administrative government was responsible for a budget of £5.8 billion, a figure representing something over 80 per cent of public expenditure in Wales. The remainder comprised spending on law and order, social security, defence, overseas services and debt interest.

All this occurred, certainly in the early days, in the teeth of Whitehall's resentment if not opposition. The prevailing attitude was reflected by Richard Crossman who confided to his diary in 1964:

> Another idiotic creation is the Department for Wales, a completely new office for Jim Griffiths and his two Parliamentary secretaries, all the result of a silly election pledge.[5]

Alongside the Welsh Office a network of outlying institutions has been spawned: the so-called quasi autonomous non-governmental organizations or quangos, referred to officially as NDPBs—non-departmental public bodies. So the Welsh Arts Council was created

[5] R. H. S. Crossman, *The Crossman Diaries*, Magnum Books, 1979, p. 63

in 1967, the Wales Tourist Board in 1969, the Sports Council for Wales in 1971, the eight (now nine) health authorities in 1974. In 1975 the Land Authority for Wales was founded, followed by the Welsh Development Agency in 1976 and the Development Board for Rural Wales in 1977.

A significant moment occurred during the late 1960s when, in response to these developments, the Transport and General Workers' Union reorganized itself on an all-Wales basis (merging its south and north Wales areas) and then joined with the National Union of Mineworkers in campaigning for a Wales Trades Union Council. This was established in 1972 in a unilateral act of defiance against the Trades Union Council in London which was forced to change its organization in England into regions by way of accommodation. Ten years later, faced with the continuing growth of the Welsh Office and superior funding for the Wales CBI, the Wales TUC secured funding for a full-time secretary and back-up staff.

It might have been thought that as a consequence of the 1979 referendum, the process of establishing new national institutions and extending the role of the Welsh Office, might have drawn to a close. In fact, the reverse occurred. Not only did both processes gain a new dynamic, but an entirely new dimension was added as post-1979 Secretaries of State for Wales demonstrated a commitment to promote autonomous industrial regeneration in Wales.

First there was an accentuated development of new national institutions, involving initially and crucially the establishment of *S4C* (the Welsh Fourth Television Channel). This was set up after a campaign of direct action at the end of which the government acknowledged that it had failed to win the 'middle ground of opinion' in Wales.

Other institutions rapidly followed in the 1980s: a Schools Curriculum Council for Wales; the Welsh Language Education Development Committee; Tai Cymru/Housing for Wales, to fund and co-ordinate the work of the expanding numbers of locally-run private housing associations; a Welsh Language Board; a Welsh Health Promotion Authority; CADW, established inside the Welsh Office to administer and promote sites of historic interest; and the Cardiff Bay Development Corporation.

In the 1990s the process continued with the creation of the Countryside Council for Wales in 1991 by merging the Welsh arms of the Countryside Commission and the Nature Conservancy Council. At the same time the work of the Manpower Services Commission was devolved to seven Welsh Training and Enterprise Councils, funded and co-ordinated from 1992 by a new Education and Training Department inside the Welsh Office. Most important of all, however, was the devolution of Higher and Further Education from the Department of Education into the control of the Welsh Office, and administered at arm's length by two new quangos: the Higher and Further Education Funding Councils.

These last two developments reflected the on-going evolution of the Welsh Office itself during the same period. The most important first step took place in the immediate aftermath of the 1979 referendum when the Welsh Office secured responsibility for a block-grant covering its expenditure responsibilities. This it negotiates each year directly with the Treasury. The Secretary of State for Wales is empowered, if necessary, to argue his case in Cabinet.

The Welsh Office now allocates the block-grant between its many areas of responsibility, ranging from education, health and housing to economic development, roads, and agriculture. In particular, it is responsible for distributing central government financial support to the eight Welsh county councils and thirty-seven districts. The forum where this is negotiated each year, with the Assembly of Welsh Counties and Council of Welsh Districts, is the Welsh Consultative Council on Local Government Finance.

Meanwhile, the Welsh Development Agency has been elaborated through the establishment of a series of subsidiary but closely related arms. Hafren Investment Finance was set up as a subsidiary in 1982 whilst Welsh Development Capital (Management) was established as a joint venture between the WDA and the Development Capital Group in 1985. Later in the 1980s a Welsh Financial Services Initiative was launched jointly by the WDA and the Welsh Office, aimed at promoting south-east Wales in particular as a major financial centre outside London.

More notable, however, was the creation of WINvest, followed in 1989 by the more elaborate Welsh Development International, with a separate board of management, to attract inward investment into Wales. In 1992, in conjunction with the Welsh Office and Welsh local authorities, this opened an office in Brussels to liaise with the European Commission.

QUANGOLAND

Nothing typifies the present government of Wales more than the appointment of former Tory MP Ian Grist, who lost his Cardiff Central seat at the General Election, to chair the South Glamorgan Health Authority. Now responsible for a £232 million annual budget, the affable Mr Grist wields far more influence over the lives of his former constituents than ever he did as a backbench MP.

Arguably his three-days-a-week, £19,285-a-year new job gives him more influence even than during his period as a junior Welsh Office Minister responsible for Health, between June 1987 and December 1990 when John Major sacked him in his first reshuffle.

In any event, Ian Grist has few illusions about the role of the backbencher. After he lost his ministerial post he refused to sit on the Welsh Affairs Select Committee, saying it would be a waste of time:

> By its nature it has the choice of interesting but lightweight single-day investigations, or undertaking research in depth into a subject such as water or tourism which is of direct interest to only a minority of Welsh MPs.[6]

Whether the Welsh health service can be placed alongside water and tourism in this context is a moot point. Certainly it featured large as an issue in the General Election in Wales, which Labour won convincingly with 49.5 per cent of the vote and twenty-seven of the thirty-eight Welsh seats (Tories six, Plaid Cymru four, and Liberal Democrats one). Yet because of their overwhelming vote in England the Tories continue to rule Wales through their grip on the Welsh Office and increasingly partisan quango appointments.

Wales's Quangoland is populated by 250 part-time salaried nominees of the Secretary of State for Wales drawing a total stipend

[6] Ian Grist: letter to the *Western Mail*, 14 December 1990

in 1991 of £1,585,000, and a further 1,429 part-time non-salaried appointees. They are made up of 1,397 men and 282 women. These figures prompted Newport West Labour MP Paul Flynn to jibe:

> Some of these quangos have budgets larger than district councils in Wales, yet these people are unelected. Welsh quangos are in reality run by TWEMS—Tory Welsh Establishment Males.[7]

Leader of the pack is undoubtedly the charismatic Welsh-speaking one-time millionaire chairman of the Welsh Development Agency, Dr Gwyn Jones. He received his appointment from the former Secretary of State for Wales, Peter Walker, after they met by chance at a dinner party. Once widely tipped as a candidate for the safe Tory seat of Clwyd North West (to succeed stalking horse Sir Anthony Meyer), in early 1992 Dr Jones was also made chairman of the BBC Council for Wales and a board member of the *S4C* Authority. These positions, if sustained, would have meant his working at least six-and-a-half days a week in Government-appointed roles for a total of £85,025 a year. In the event, and after protests, it was announced that he would have his hours cut at the WDA from four days a week to two-and-a-half, and his WDA salary reduced from £64,975 a year to £40,610.

Cardiff Bay Development Corporation chairman and former Tory candidate Geoffrey Inkin is also chairman of the Land Authority for Wales with a joint salary of £59,500. The chairman of Tai Cymru/Housing for Wales, John Allen, earns £27,250 in that role and a further £8,395 as deputy chairman of the Land Authority for Wales. The deputy chairman (honorarium £7,703) of Tai Cymru, until he was elected Conservative MP for Brecon and Radnor at the 1992 General Election, was the Cardiff solicitor Jonathan Evans. The chairman of the Development Board for Rural Wales, Glyn Davies, earns £29,835 and another £5,900 as a member of the Wales Tourist Board. He also sits on the Welsh Development Agency board, although he is not paid for that role.

[7] *Western Mail*, 3 March 1992

Another key-member of Welsh quangoland is Sir Donald Walters, a former chairman of the Welsh Conservative Party. He is currently chairman of the Council of the University College of Wales, Cardiff, deputy chairman of the Welsh Development Agency, and a board member of the Development Board for Rural Wales.

The day the 1992 General Election was called, the Welsh Office released the names of Wales's newest quango, the Higher Education Funding Council. Controlling a budget of some £150 million this is responsible for the six University of Wales colleges plus the University of Glamorgan (formerly the Polytechnic of Wales), Bangor Normal College, Trinity College Carmarthen, the Welsh Agricultural College, and the Welsh College of Music and Drama. It is responsible for their grants, opening and closing departments, determining student numbers and the balance of spending between teaching and research.

The chairman of the new council is Sir Idris Pearce, from Dorking, Surrey, president of the Royal Institute of Chartered Surveyors and chairman of English Estates, a property tycoon. He stood for the Tories in Neath in the 1959 General Election.

Members of the Council are Professor John Cadogan, director of Research with British Petroleum in London; Sir Sam Edwards, Cavendish Professor of Physics at Cambridge; Sir Philip Jones, chairman of the Total Oil Holding and the Electricity Council; Dr Alfred Morris, director of Bristol Polytechnic; and Richard Griffiths, Professor of French at King's College, London.

The sole female member of the Council is Dr Ann Robinson, formerly a lecturer in politics at University College, Cardiff. In the mid-1980s she was nominated by the Welsh Office as Wales' representative on the European Commission's advisory Economic and Social Committee. Partly on the strength of that appointment she later became head of the Institute of Directors' policy unit. In 1979 she was the Tory's Euro-candidate in South-East Wales.

There are four Welsh-based members of the Council. Michael Griffiths, a financier, is also chairman of Clwyd Health Authority and the Countryside Council for Wales. He is Vice-Lord Lieutenant of Clwyd. Alan Cox is chairman and chief executive of the Cardiff-based firm, Allied Steel and Wire. Dr Brynley Roberts is the National Librarian at Aberystwyth. Chief executive and board

member of the Council is Professor John Andrews, forr
of the Law Department at the University College
Aberystwyth, and now a civil servant.

In the wake of the 1992 General Election Torfaen's Labou...
Paul Murphy put down a House of Commons Early Day Motion accusing the Secretary of State for Wales, David Hunt, of packing Welsh quangos with Conservative place-people. This drew an unrepentant response from the newly-elected Conservative MP for Clwyd North-West, Rod Richards:

> The Secretary of State and his predecessors have always looked for quality people to sit on them. If the Labour Party are saying that all these hand-picked, high-calibre, top-drawer people are Conservatives, then they are paying us a compliment.[8]

Quite apart from side-stepping the fundamental question of democracy, such debating points ignore two outstanding features of quango appointments: their often arbitrary and idiosyncratic character; and the way some individuals find themselves appointed to more than one body, creating in the process an inter-meshed network of unaccountable influence.

One illustration is the composition of the Welsh Arts Council, responsible in 1992-3 for a budget of £12,886,242. Influential members of its seventeen-strong committee are closely involved in other areas of Welsh public life. So, for example, Hugh Hudson Davies, a former director of Coopers and Lybrand, is also a member of the boards of the Cardiff Bay Development Corporation, Powys Health Authority and the Welsh National Opera. The chairman, Mathew Prichard, millionaire grandson of Agatha Christie, is also chairman of the Cardiff Bay Arts Trust and vice-president of the Council of the National Museum of Wales. He was appointed chairman of the Arts Council in 1986 by his cousin, the former Secretary of State for Wales, Nicholas Edwards, now Lord Crickhowell.

The vice-chairman, David Bowen Lewis, another millionaire, is a former director of the Wales Crafts Council, and a former member of the Prince of Wales Award Committee of the Welsh Design

[8] *Western Mail*, 12 June 1992

Council. Another Welsh Arts Council member is Dr Ann Robinson who, as stated above, was appointed in early 1992 to the new Higher Education Council for Wales, and is also the Welsh representative on the EC's Economic and Social Committee.

Though a sub-committee of the Arts Council of Great Britain, the Welsh Arts Council is firmly within the control of the Welsh Office. About half its membership in 1992 had been appointed as a result of direct contact with a Welsh Office Minister. So, for instance, shortly before the 1992 Election Mrs Sherilyn Bankes had accompanied her husband, a stockbroker, to a Conservative function in Mold where she met the Secretary of State for Wales, David Hunt. Not long afterwards she received a letter inviting her to become a member of the Welsh Arts Council. Mrs Bankes, who is American and formerly a commercial lawyer with British Steel, has a keen interest in the arts. She is a founder-member of the Friends of Theatr Clwyd and edits their newsletter. But for that chance meeting in the Spring of 1992, however, there is little likelihood that she would have become a member of the Welsh Arts Council.

The other main route to membership is first to join one of the Council's subject committees, specializing in drama, music, literature, dance, film, art or craft. Each of these committees is chaired by a full member of the Arts Council. But most of the remaining members are co-opted on the advice of already existing members and the Welsh Arts Council's full-time staff. From time to time co-opted people who make a significant contribution are put forward to the Welsh Office as candidates for full membership. This is the main way over the past ten years that non-Conservative supporters have become full members of the Arts Council.

In 1992 the political make-up of the Council's membership was estimated at eight Conservative supporters, four Labour, three Liberal Democrat and two Plaid Cymru. In a country where the Conservative Party regularly secures less than 30 per cent of the vote, if you're not a Conservative supporter it can be a tortuous business becoming a full member of the Welsh Arts Council. Jane Davidson, a former actress with a post-graduate qualification in drama, was a co-opted member of the Welsh Arts Council's Drama Committee in the late-1980s. She was also a Cardiff City Labour councillor and at the time her name was put forward to the Welsh Office for full membership of the Arts Council she was on the short-list for nomination as Labour's Parliamentary candidate for Cardiff Central. Surprise, surprise, her Arts Council candidature was at first blocked by the then Conservative MP for Cardiff Central and Welsh Office Under-Secretary, none other than Ian Grist. Later, however, after she had failed to win the Cardiff Central nomination, her name was resubmitted and she became a full Welsh Arts Council member in 1990.

LOCAL GOVERNMENT

The march of Welsh quangoland has occurred to a great extent at the expense of local government. Tai Cymru/Housing for Wales, with a budget now in excess of £100 million a year, has established itself largely in place of the thirty-seven district councils whose main role used to be housing.

The eight Welsh counties are witnessing the erosion of their main function, education, on two fronts: with further education and strategic planning being centralized into the Welsh Office and the Schools Curriculum and Further Education Funding Councils; and with their management of secondary education being cut away by local management of schools and by some entirely opting out of their control.

One consequence has been for all parties in Wales to agree that the counties and districts should merge into a single tier of around twenty-five most-purpose authorities.

There can be little doubt, however, that this will result in a significant diminution of local democratic control. As far as education is concerned, the former chief executive of Gwynedd County Council, Ioan Bowen Rees, has remarked that superficially it might seem that schools were gaining more freedom. But he added:

> Once a substantial number have opted out, school governors will probably find that democratically elected education committees are like Santa Claus compared with the Welsh Office and the Treasury; and already it is easier to become a

governor by knowing the right people than by democratic election. The centralization of major services not only reduces democratic control and threatens co-ordination. It threatens the very viability and clout of multi-purpose authorities since their great merit is that the organization as a whole is greater than the sum of its parts.[9]

More immediately, reducing the number of councils reduces the number of elected councillors. The 1974 local government reorganization, which reduced the number of elected major authorities in Wales from 181 to forty-five, halved the number of councillors. Cutting the number of councils once more, this time from forty-five to twenty-five, will have a comparable result.

In any event the progressive erosion of local government's financial discretion, combined with the loss of functions, is already having a negative impact on the quality of democracy. This can be seen most clearly in the increasing tendency for councillors in all parts of Wales to be elected unopposed. Where they have little chance of winning, the political parties tend not to stand. Thus the Labour Party has retreated from much of rural Wales; the Conservatives contest only some of the anglicized margins of Wales, elsewhere leaving a clear run for Independents; the Liberal Democrats fight patchily in Conwy and Cardiff; while Plaid Cymru concentrates on the Valleys and its *Bro Gymraeg* heartland.

There is, of course, a case for merging the counties and districts into a single tier, to unify complementary functions and cut out waste and confusion. It never made sense, for instance, for the districts to collect rubbish but the counties to make strategic decisions about its disposal; nor that responsibility for the homeless (the districts) should be split from social services (the counties). Yet if a most-purpose single tier makes sense in these terms, effective democracy requires that strategic decision-making be accountable at the all-Wales level, while real local concerns be dealt with at a level much closer to the people.

As well as the districts and counties, Wales has 765 relatively powerless Community Councils. There is a great deal of scope for

[9] Ioan Bowen Rees, 'Local Government Reorganization in Wales', *Planet* 91 (Aberystwyth), Feb/March 1992

these to be reduced in number, but to take on real powers in relation to planning, housing, education, environmental concerns like recycling, and advising the police on law and order. Further, they could have real rather than ineffective advisory planning powers enabling them to restrain unwanted developments. They could be entitled to have representation on housing associations in their area and a liaison role with the most-purpose authorities in this field. There is potential, too, for them to participate in the governing bodies of schools.

Although Labour, Liberal Democrat and Plaid Cymru all have developed policies along these lines, the Conservatives have pressed the case for a single tier of local government in isolation of improving democratic arrangements either above or below. In light of this it is instructive to ask why the Conservatives opted for a single-tier of authorities based upon the districts rather than the counties. It is tempting to conclude simply that in the wake of the 1991 district council elections the Labour Party lost its control of the Council of Welsh Districts, while remaining in control of the Assembly of Welsh Counties. Nonetheless, there are three strong arguments for creating a single tier of Welsh local government around a smaller rather than larger number of authorities—arguments that should, on the face of it, appeal to a Conservative Secretary of State for Wales.

The first, and perhaps most important, is efficiency. All objective studies have made the case for local authority populations to be nearer those of the counties than the districts. Now that housing has been largely stripped from the districts, by the all-Wales quango Tai Cymru/Housing for Wales, the most important local authority functions (entailing some 85 per cent of local expenditure) are run by the counties. These include education, social services, roads, fire services and strategic planning. They connect directly in terms of boundaries and population with two other vital services outside elected local government—health, run by the nine (Welsh Office-nominated) health authorities; and training, run by seven (Welsh Office-directed) Training and Enterprise Councils.

Indeed, there are strong indications that, as part of the creation of a single-tier of twenty-five local authorities the Welsh Office is planning to transfer responsibility for the eight county social service departments and their combined £310 million-a-year budget to the nominated Health Authorities. In early 1992 a delegation of Welsh Office civil servants visited Northern Ireland to study the way social services are administered there, by the Province's Health Authorities. As the Assembly of Welsh Counties deputy chairman, John Howard Davies, put it:

> We are going to see social services transferred to the health authorities. This stands out clearly to me. It is because the health authorities are being denuded of their hospitals as they gain trust status, and their workload is therefore getting less and less. This Government's aim is to transfer many of the services from local government to Government-appointed quangos.[10]

The second argument for creating a single tier around a smaller, rather than larger number of authorities—and one that again should appeal particularly to the Conservatives—is cost. In pressing the case for building a single tier on their own boundaries both the counties and districts hired independent consultants to come up with comparative costs and savings. Taking a mean point between their estimates, a single tier of eight authorities would save about £30 million a year, and 13 authorities about £20 million. But twenty-three to twenty-five authorities, the preferred Conservative solution, would actually cost about £5 million more.

The third argument is political. If the Welsh Office opted for eight authorities (or perhaps thirteen, so that a return could be made to some of the old counties like Pembrokeshire, Anglesey and Monmouthshire) the line could be held much more easily against the need for an elected all-Wales strategic tier of government. A small number of larger authorities could carry out the strategic functions of local government in a way that the larger number are unlikely to be able or be allowed to do. For instance, on top of the likely removal of social services from democratic control, it has been suggested that instead of having twenty-three or twenty-five directors of education, the proposed single tier of authorities

[10] *Western Mail*, 13 May 1992

would come together in loose groups and appoint one among their number as the lead authority for the area.

All this leaves the way wide open for the logical solution: an elected all-Wales Assembly to be responsible for strategic policy—on health, education, social services, economic planning, fire services, the police, and the rest.

So why have the Conservatives chosen a district-based solution rather than one built on the counties, so leaving the way open for the creation of a Welsh Assembly? Doubtless, the answer must be, in the first instance, because they believe they can easily resist demands for an Assembly. But secondly, and more fundamentally, the suspicion must be because they believe they can more easily control a larger number of weaker authorities than a smaller number of more powerful ones. The way will be clear to turn local authorities into executive agencies rather than autonomous councils with real discretionary powers. As Ioan Bowen Rees concluded:

> A reorganization led by a Secretary of State whose party is in the minority in Wales is a recipe for instability. Reorganization is a job for a Welsh Assembly, democratically elected by the people of Wales but advised by as independent and consensually minded a commission as can be appointed . . .
>
> But there is no urgency. What is urgent is reform of the system of central government that gave us the Poll Tax, only to have to unravel it at a cost exceeding a billion pounds. Neither can you reform local government properly without reforming central government at the same time: the relations between them are crucial to proper democratic accountability . . .
>
> A Welsh Assembly is part of the package of essential central government reform. Until that Assembly is in place, local government reform will be little more than a charade.[11]

[11] Ioan Bowen Rees, op. cit.

BROADCASTING

One essential condition for a sense of Welsh citizenship comparable with that in Scotland is the development of a comparable integrated internal communications network. English-speaking Welsh people, especially, are caught in a special dilemma in this respect. On one side of them is a surging mass of English/American culture channelled overwhelmingly through centralized London-based television; on the other is a vivid, if less powerful, Welsh-language culture channelled through *S4C*. The result is at least two entirely separate arenas for communication within Wales—and three if you divide the English-language audience between those who point their television aerials towards English-based transmitters and those who tune in to BBC Wales and HTV Wales.

Little wonder therefore that the innate Welsh tendency to tribalism and fragmentation based on locality has flourished at the expense of any all-Wales consciousness, let alone citizenship. It can be argued that the development of *Radio Cymru* in the late 1970s, followed by *S4C* in the 1980s, has provided the Welsh-language community with the basis of a fully-integrated communications network. In doing so it has also pointed the way forward for the English-language media in Wales.

It is difficult to over-emphasise the importance of the establishment of *S4C* in 1982, not just in increasing the quantity and range of Welsh broadcasting, but as an institution in itself. Writing a year after the new channel was created, HTV's then Controller of Programmes, Geraint Talfan Davies, described it as:

> . . . a national service, not an adjunct to another service, not a regional gloss, not an embellishment for a metropolitan schedule, but a free-standing comprehensive service that stands or falls on its own—a buck that cannot be passed up the line to London.
>
> It is that national context that elevates our function as much and perhaps more than the language in which it is done. It is that national context that prevents mixture of local and international material from seeming bizarre. Sunday opening

> and El Salvador can stand cheek by jowl without raising an eyebrow.[12]

More than this, however, Talfan Davies went on to describe the impact the new channel was having on English-language television in Wales. To begin with, the clearing from HTV Wales of its Welsh-language output had allowed the company's programmes in English to rise from three-and-a-half hours a week to seven. The English-language news service had expanded from one-and-a-half hours to three-and-a-half hours a week, and more financial and human resources were being devoted to English programming. The essential motivation, he conceded, was political:

> The goodwill of the majority that is needed to sustain *S4C* must be guaranteed by providing the best possible English-language service for Wales.
>
> But conversely *S4C* is an asset to English-language broadcasting because it provides benchmarks in terms of function within Wales that can only be of benefit to those working in English. Our English-language programmes have to be placed within an ITV schedule. Our role will inevitably be different from that of *S4C*. But the continued existence of *S4C* with its national character and function should be an inspiration and bulwark against a drift into provincialism in English-language programming. And that is a real danger when regionalism in England is weak and provides no convincing countervailing force against the centralist perceptions of British television organizations.[13]

The quantity and range of English-language programming on HTV Wales and BBC Wales increased gradually through the 1980s. By the end of the decade both were producing around eight hours a week. But this still fell far short of a comprehensive service. Overwhelmingly made up of news, current affairs and sport, there

[12] Geraint Talfan Davies, 'S4C: New Opportunities and Responsibilities' in J. Barry Jones (ed), *Bilingualism and the Media: Canada and Wales* (University College of Wales, Cardiff), 1984

[13] Ibid

was very little documentary programming and very little home-produced drama on a regular basis.

Worse still, what was being produced was to a very great extent being duplicated, with similar news programmes, farming magazines, political reports from Parliament, even current affairs, being transmitted by HTV Wales and BBC Wales. Sometimes transmission times clashed as well. It raises the question whether in a situation where there is relatively little home-produced English-language output from Wales, such duplication can be justified. The parlous state of Welsh English-language television, especially when compared with the service provided by *S4C*, was summarized by Geraint Talfan Davies in 1991, by which time he had joined BBC Wales as Controller:

> There is a problem. About 85 per cent of our present eight hours a week of English output is news, current affairs and sport, that is reactive programming, or topical programming geared to specific events. That leaves only 15 per cent to reflect upon every other aspect of Welsh life and it is not good enough. We have to find more hours for English-language programming so that we can provide a more complete reflection of the political, economic, cultural and artistic life of Wales.[14]

Geraint Talfan Davies's response was to commit BBC Wales to producing ten hours of programming a week, with significant improvement in the output of English-language documentary and drama output. This had an immediate impact on HTV Wales which, under the pressure of the renewal of its franchise, made a similar commitment.

Both BBC and HTV will have many problems in achieving these targets, however. BBC Wales, faced with financial cutbacks, has a continual problem of access to network slots and budgets. HTV has the problem of funding programmes when, under the Channel 3 arrangements, it has to pay a £20.5 million-a-year levy to the Treasury for the privilege of broadcasting at all.

[14] 'See for Yourself', BBC Wales (Cardiff), 7 January 1991

So, though there have been improvements to the amount and, to some extent, quality of English-language television in Wales, there is as yet nowhere near the range, diversity and integration of the service provided for Welsh-language viewers by *S4C*.

In this situation it is instructive to look at what the Welsh Language Board said in 1989, responding to the Government's White Paper on 'Broadcasting in the 1990s: Competition, Choice and Quality', produced prior to the legislation that established Channel 3:

> Increasingly, a nation is becoming what television says it is. People's perceptions of themselves are developed through these external influences rather than through personal and shared experiences. For Wales these external influences are more likely to come from Los Angeles and London than they are to come from Cardiff and they threaten the sense of being Welsh and therefore the long-term survival of the Welsh language . . .
>
> Any plan for safeguarding Welsh broadcasting must cater equally for the interests of Welsh-speakers and non-Welsh-speakers. The language may be a manifestation of our separate culture as Welsh people or it may be one end result of other deep-rooted differences.
>
> Whatever the truth, the language cannot survive in a nation where non-Welsh-speakers do not continue to feel themselves to be different from the other people of the United Kingdom. Television is the prime influence in creating the cultural climate which can nurture or destroy these differences . . . [15]

The Welsh Language Board went on to press the case for equivalent treatment on television within Wales for the English as the Welsh language. This, it argued, could only mean the setting up of an English-language channel for Wales along similar lines to *S4C*.

A big question, of course, is the extent to which the aspiration for a separate, English-language, channel is held by the English-speaking Welsh themselves. The only hard evidence—a poll

[15] Welsh Language Board, Letter to the Secretary of State for Wales, 7 March 1989

conducted by the *Western Mail* in February 1990—indicates strong support. The response to the question 'Would you be in favour of Wales having its own television channel to serve English-speakers in the same way that S4C serves Welsh-speakers?' was:

	%
In favour	73
Against	17
Don't know	11

Of course, the question was in one sense superficial in that it did not make clear that the creation of such a channel, with more home-originated programmes at peak hours, would inevitably result in a deprivation effect. That is to say, Welsh viewers would be deprived to some extent of programmes coming from London, though depending on the precise arrangements that were made for an English-language channel, such programmes could be rescheduled in the same way that Channel 4 UK programmes are rescheduled on *S4C*.

Whatever the strength of such arguments it is plain that there is a strong inter-relationship between the Welsh and English languages in the development of television in Wales. Such improvements to the English-language service that have occurred, certainly during the 1980s, came about in response to the advances made in Welsh-language television. Equally, as the Welsh Language Board has made clear, safeguarding these advances now requires a much improved and more stable environment for English-language television.

What this means, as the Language Board has also argued, is the creation of an English-language television channel for Wales.

How practical could this be? The Welsh Language Board, from the perspective of 1989, pressed the case for the new Channel 3—that is, HTV's—being remoulded to create the service. It should, the Board said, operate on similar lines to *S4C*, taking programmes from the BBC and being the only channel on which home-produced English-language programmes were transmitted.

However, now that Channel 3 is well on the way to being set up, a more sustainable approach might be to choose BBC 2 Wales instead. BBC 2 Wales is already used regularly as an opt-out channel to broadcast Welsh programming in English. There is no technical reason why it could not be developed as the English-language Welsh channel—Channel 2 Wales. The *S4C* analogy could still be followed, but with the Channel 3 franchise holder in Wales, that is HTV, required to provide Channel 2 with a set number of hours per week of locally-made programmes. This would leave the Channel 3 airwaves in Wales open entirely for network programming, so making it commercially more attractive and, to that extent, more able to produce and commission quality home-produced programmes for Channel 2 Wales.

Further into the 1990s there may be twin pressures on BBC 2 UK:

(i) to become an arts, music and sports channel geared to attracting sponsorship;
(ii) to become a federalized channel, carrying regional news and current affairs, so freeing BBC 1 to carry more perceived popular programming to compete head-on with Channel 3 and the satellite channels.

Both pressures make it easier to envisage BBC 2 being used for the English-language Channel 2 Wales option. There is a precedent in Sweden for this approach. There, Channel 2 has been turned into a regional channel with a brief of enhancing regional variety and identity within the country, leaving Channel 1 as the more popular 'entertainment' channel. The result has been to increase the audience for the Swedish Channel 2.

In a broadcasting environment where there will be a multiplicity of channels before the end of the 1990s, it is reasonable to hope that an English-language channel based firmly on the national community of Wales, alongside *S4C*, would have as good a chance as its competitors, and probably better, of attracting a significant audience share.

The only serious track-record in this field—*Radio Cymru*, Radio Wales, and *S4C*—provides solid grounds for optimism. Radio Wales is the best template. After an uncertain beginning in the late 1970s, it took most of the 1980s to find a distinctive, Welsh voice in the English language. Uncontrovertibly it has now achieved one, and in the process a large slice of the Welsh listening audience. After Radio 1 it is the most popular radio channel in Wales, with an audience reach of 435,000 a week, a figure well in excess of 20 per cent.

Establishing an English-language channel for Wales may be a medium-term goal. It will probably require the creation, first, of an elected Welsh Assembly to mobilize the political will. Yet if the promotion of a mature democratic culture in Wales is the objective, an English-language channel should be held firmly in view while at the same time bringing pressure on BBC Wales and HTV Wales to improve, and schedule in a more complementary way, their English-language output.

THE WELSH POLICY-MAKING PROCESS

As has been described, there is now a large Welsh bureaucratic state structure in existence. The Welsh Office, together with its increasing array of subordinate bodies, the quangos, has charge of the commanding heights of the Welsh economy and society.

Welsh Office civil servants run the equivalent of a dozen English ministries, with briefs covering Economic and Regional Planning (four divisions); Industry (three divisions); Agriculture (three divisions); Legal Affairs; Establishment (six divisions); Finance (three divisions); National Health Service (twelve divisions); Housing, Health and Social Services (six divisions); Highways (four divisions); Transport, Planning and the Environment (six divisions); and Training and Education (six divisions).

These wide-ranging responsibilities are the subject of just eight question-days a year in the House of Commons (each of some 30 minutes), one Welsh-day debate a year and no more than four sittings of the Welsh Grand Committee. In addition, since the early 1980s there has been in existence the Select Committee on Welsh Affairs. However, its investigations have tended to be wide-ranging and superficial, making little impact on the Welsh Office's administration. Moreover, under a Conservative administration it has operated with the dual difficulty of having an Opposition majority and members increasingly reluctant to serve on it, for instance the former Conservative MP for Cardiff Central, Ian Grist.

In England, where each of the Welsh Office's departments is the responsibility of a separate ministry, they are much more effectively followed and scrutinized. They each have their own Select Committee, have a separate full period of questions on the floor of the House of Commons and are the subject of several debates each session. One group of English MPs concentrates on health, another on education and so on, and these members can watch closely over the work of the relevant ministry.

For Welsh affairs, however, one question-time every four weeks or so has to suffice for all the activities of the Welsh Office. As a result it is not worthwhile for Welsh MPs to specialize in Welsh policy areas: the effect being to give civil servants in Wales greater freedom of action than is permitted those administering the same functions in England. When the Commission on the Constitution was taking evidence in Wales in 1969, Sir Goronwy Daniel, then Permanent Under-Secretary at the Welsh Office, was asked if there was a danger of an élite civil service controlling the affairs of Wales. He replied:

> I think dangers of that kind might arise for two reasons. One is that if accountability is only to Westminster, then the amount of time which can be made available is limited, and the amount of interest shown by members generally is also limited.
>
> The other factor is that, as the functions of the Secretary of State grow, it becomes necessary for him to delegate more and more work to officials. If the Secretary of State had full responsibility for education, for agriculture, for child care and for various other things one can think of, the volume of work would be pretty considerable.[16]

Since Sir Goronwy made this point all these functions, and many more, have come under Welsh Office control. Moreover, as has been listed above, the Welsh Office has spawned many outposts of administration which, together with local government, comprise an unaccountable network of largely invisible policy-making. So

[16] Commission on the Constitution, 'Minutes of Evidence', vol 1, Wales (HMSO, 1970), para. 14

much so that during the 1980s two semi-private outside organizations came into being in an effort to create an informal consultative network. These were the Institute of Welsh Affairs, which commissions reports on aspects of Welsh policy and publishes an annual Welsh Economic Review, and the St David's Forum. The latter meets for a weekend once or twice a year, drawing together civil servants and quango personnel, local government officers, leaders of business and industry, trade unionists, together with representatives from the Welsh media. It is noteworthy, however, that politicians are not invited and that all discussions are strictly 'off-the-record'.

After nearly thirty years of development, following the foundation of the Welsh Office, it is by now the interaction between the bodies and people involved, as much as the institutions themselves, that make up a formidable layer of administrative but effectively unaccountable Welsh government. As one study of the process judged:

> This network of consultative government in Wales ought now to be seen and understood as an important institution in the government of Wales. It may be regarded as an effective supplement to the formal institutions, though essentially informal, flexible and largely private, and to some extent 'depoliticized', that is removed from the arena of political conflict.
>
> Arguably, the value of the network lies in just these qualities. This is a narrow, executive view of consultation, seeing it as to do with administration and execution. However, it is also to do with policy formulation by way of modification in implementation, allocation of resources and feed-back. Hence there is scope for a more expansive view of consultation, and a case for developing the network into a more open and inclusive institution of inter-governmental relations. The logic of the working of the system points to the value of an all-Wales elected body . . . [17]

[17] P. J. Madgwick and Mari James, 'Government by Consultation: The Case of Wales', Centre for the Study of Public Policy (University of Strathclyde), 1979, p. 41

This view was put forward in 1979, at the outset of a long peri
of minority Conservative government in Wales. After twelve years the Conservatives were willing to concede the point as far as including in their 1992 Election manifesto a proposal for a nominated Welsh Economic Council, chaired by the Secretary of State.

This will formally, rather than informally, bring round the table representatives from the local authorities, Wales CBI, Wales TUC, the Welsh Development Agency, Development Board for Rural Wales, Wales Tourist Board, the Training and Enterprise Councils, and the new Further and Higher Education Funding Councils. All this, according to the Conservative 1992 Election manifesto, would be to 'ensure greater cohesion and a more united effort on the part of the Principality's major employers' and employees' organizations'.

It will, of course, be a case of Wales's quangoland coming of age. Meanwhile, the Conservative administration at the Welsh Office, together with its increasingly compliant bureaucracy, continues to pursue an audacious interventionist strategy, relatively independent of Whitehall, of promoting autonomous Welsh economic regeneration.

For Nicholas Edwards, Secretary of State for Wales between 1979 and 1987, this entailed a commitment to use the Welsh Office to establish links between industry, the venture capital market and the University of Wales, with the Welsh Development Agency in a supportive role. Peter Walker, who succeeded Edwards in the wake of the 1987 Election, maintained the approach. It is clear, for example, that his insistence on a separate Welsh committee of the University Funding Council that succeeded the University Grants Committee, was part of this strategy. David Hunt, who replaced Walker in 1990, took the policy even further by overseeing the complete administrative devolution of higher education to the Welsh Office and the creation of the free-standing Higher Education and Further Education Funding Councils for Wales.

The main thrust, however, was carried by targeting resources on the Cardiff Bay Development Project (involving expenditure in excess of £2 billion during the 1990s), the Valleys Initiative (with a more modest, mainly re-cycled, £500 million) and completing the

5. One result was to widen the prosperity gap between th Wales and the remainder of the country, especially s and the rural hinterland where farmers experienced a steeply declining incomes. Yet successive Conservative rations at the Welsh Office managed to finesse their policies with a gloss of partnership and consensus that more often than not put the majority Opposition on the defensive. The master was, of course, Peter Walker who, looking back on his Welsh Office tenure between 1987 and 1990, contrasted his approach with the Thatcherite reliance on free-market forces across the border.

> What we achieved in Wales as a result of close government co-operation with industry, councils and trade unions does underscore the weakness of our post-war performance in the rest of the country... Britain, with its free trade attitude belonging to another century, adopted under Margaret an arms-length relationship between government and industry.[18]

Over fifteen, and perhaps twenty years, Tory administrations at the Welsh Office have been given a free hand to remodel Wales according to the dictates of a market-orientated private capitalist ethic, albeit one that is slightly more emollient than in England. Key community institutions, most notably the health service, and the services administered by local government—education and housing to name only the most important—are taking a back seat (and in some cases being dismantled) while expenditure priorities forge ahead in other directions. The full significance of the failure to achieve an Assembly in 1979 can now be seen as allowing control of the Welsh Office and its quangos to fall into the hands of an unrepresentative, democratically unaccountable, Conservative administration.

[18] P. Walker, *Staying Power: An Autobiography* (London, 1991), p. 212

Wales, pronounced David Hunt in the wake of the 1992 General Election, was on course to take its place among the most dynamic economies in the new Europe:

> We have worked long and hard to put Wales firmly on the map of our new Europe–in its own right and as a full constituent part of the UK–for Europe's economic and political foundations are in regions such as Wales.[19]

He was referring to a remarkable initiative, begun by Peter Walker, to integrate Wales with some of the leading regional European economies, the so-called 'Four Motor Regions'–Baden-Wurttemberg, Lombardy, Rhone-Alpes and Catalunya. Formal agreements had either been signed, or were being negotiated with all four, entailing technology transfer in the industrial field, joint ventures, investment such as the new Bosch (Baden-Wurttemberg) alternator plant outside Cardiff, and reciprocal cultural and academic exchanges. After listing these achievements David Hunt added:

> Wales is already beginning to play a leading role on the European stage and I am determined to see this develop, not just for the benefit of our economy, but for the enhancement of our national life.[20]

Such aspirations simultaneously present a problem and a democratic opportunity. Precisely how is Wales to play the 'leading role on the European stage' that David Hunt claims? Compared with the other larger European Community states the United Kingdom is the only one not to have developed a democratic regional structure. This raises the immediate problem of how the United Kingdom is to be represented on the new Committee of the Regions that is being established under the Maastricht Treaty on European Union. A potentially influential body, this is seen by

[19] *The Observer*, 31 May 1992
[20] Ibid

Euro-federalists as an embryonic upper chamber for the European Parliament. Its continental membership will be elected representatives from regional Parliaments, Assemblies and Councils across Europe. The United Kingdom's twenty-four representatives, however, will be a low-grade mixture of officials from the English local authority associations and civil servants from the Welsh Office, Scottish Office and Northern Ireland Office.

For centralized nation-states like the United Kingdom, 'Regions' are undoubtedly a subversive idea, one that is often put alongside the supra-national structures of the EC as threatening their integrity. Yet the idea is spreading.

Twenty years ago West Germany—a federation—was the only country within the European Community to have strong regions. Since then Belgium, Italy, Spain, and France have all introduced regional structures that conform to the standard set by the Assembly of European Regions, established at Strasbourg in 1985. This declares a Region to be a 'level of government immediately below the central government with political representation guaranteed by the existence of an elected Regional Council, or failing this, by an association or body constituted at Regional level by the local authorities at the level immediately below'.

On this definition Wales qualifies, since it is represented at the all-Wales level by the Assembly of Welsh Counties. The irony, however, is that the eight Welsh counties are soon to disappear.

The Council of Europe defines a Region as 'a territory which constitutes from a geographical point of view a clear-cut entity whose population possesses certain shared features and wishes to safeguard the resulting specific identity and to develop it with the object of stimulating cultural, social and political progress'. On this basis the European Community, excluding the United Kingdom, already has some seventy-eight regions with elected authorities. Over the next twenty years their number is destined to increase with, for instance, six new ones being added from Portugal. There is talk in France of redrawing some of the boundaries of its twenty-one mainland regions, merging some to make them stronger—for instance Haute and Basse Normandie—and generally making them conform more accurately with historical and cultural identities. Together with the process of closer integration underway within the European Community as a whole, it is hard to see how the sole remaining large unitary state, the United Kingdom, can remain untouched by such developments.

The battleground will be the concept of subsidiarity, enshrined in the December 1991 Maastricht Treaty, which affirms the member states' resolution:

> . . . to continue the process of creating an ever closer union among the peoples of Europe, in which decisions are taken as closely as possible to the citizen in accordance with the principle of subsidiarity.

The term is, of course, a contested idea, but generally it is accepted as meaning that decisions should not be taken by a higher body when they can effectively be taken by a lower one. So, for example, one of Britain's EC Commissioners, Sir Leon Brittan, declared:

> If the EC is to prove a liberating influence and not a centralizing and corporatist one, we must further develop and apply the (subsidiarity) principle that decisions should be taken at the lowest appropriate level: as close as possible, that is, to the people who are affected by them.[21]

This immediately raises the question: which is the lowest appropriate level? For the British government the answer is clear: the EC member states. It is a position that can be sustained by a reading of the new Article 3b, inserted into the Treaty of Rome by the Treaty agreed at Maastricht:

> In areas which do not fall within its exclusive competence, the Community shall take action, in accordance with the principle of subsidiarity, only if and so far as the objectives of the proposed action cannot be sufficiently achieved by the Member States and can therefore, by reason of the scale or effects of the proposed action, be better achieved by the Community.

[21] Sir Leon Brittan, Granada Lecture, November 1989

This clause plainly leaves it to each of the Member States to determine how subsidiarity applies in their case. How this will be worked through will reflect the constitutional arrangements in each of the Member States. So while the British Government is likely to invoke subsidiarity against Brussels, the German Lander will use it against Bonn, arguing powerfully for a new form of German federalism that institutionalizes links with the Community. Indeed, in November 1990 the German Bundesraat, the Upper Chamber representing the Lander, unanimously resolved to demand a greater say in the process of European integration. Their resolution called for a 'strengthened subsidiarity principle', with the Lander having special institutional representation at Community level.

There is no doubt that this approach is supported by the European Commission. Its President, Jacques Delors, has supported it many times, for instance in a speech to the Bavarian Parliament in May 1992, entitled 'Towards European Union—A Community of peoples, states and regions'. In it he dwelt at length on the principle of subsidiarity, acknowledging that it meant different things in different parts of Europe, but emphasizing the role of the regions in building European integration:

> The introduction of the principle of subsidiarity in the treaties of the Community signifies, for states having federal constitutions, a first step towards the creation of a third level of responsibility, after the community and the nation states, composed of Lander and regions.
>
> In this respect I know what the Lander want. Besides the European Parliament they want a regional chamber, comparable to the Bundesraat, which will give the regions genuine rights of participation.

A paper produced by the right-wing Institute of Economic Affairs in 1990 warned that even if the British Government succeeded at Maastricht in negotiating 'a tight definition' of subsidiarity—as indeed emerged—this would 'offer only limited protection against the tide of Community legislation'. And it added:

> There is a real danger that a broad definition of subsidiarity could generate a 'Westminster By-pass' problem. For many years the Commission has been anxious to build up its relations with regions and local government in the Community. Subsidiarity could provide a justification for a substantial extension of that policy . . .[22]

If we are to recover the widening democratic deficit that has long been the reality within Britain's political culture, and is now becoming all too apparent at the European Community level as well, we must indeed generate the 'Westminster By-pass' that an elected Welsh Assembly would create for us to Europe. Who can deny that the Welsh Office and its quangos now constitute a significant layer of government much closer to the people than Whitehall? Who, therefore, can reasonably argue that it should not be subjected to the European Community's subsidiarity principle?

THE DEMOCRATIC CHALLENGE

The rapidly evolving European institutional framework is providing a twenty-first century perspective on what has long been a twentieth-century reality: that to become a truly democratic culture we must inject elected responsibility and impetus into the level of Welsh administrative government we already have.

When I think about the prospects for an elected Welsh Assembly being achieved in the 1990s, two meetings I have had in the past few years invariably come to mind. Both were with politicians prominent in their own countries though little known in Wales.

The first was with the Prime Minister of Euskadi, the Basque Country, Jose Antonio Atdanza Garro. I met him in his impressive mansion near the heart of the inland capital of Vitoria in company with a delegation from the Scottish Constitutional Convention. We were on what is called a 'fact-finding mission', investigating the Spanish federal system that has been put in place in the years since Franco's death in 1975. Our meeting with the Prime Minister was supposed to last half-an-hour, but it went on for three hours, into the gathering dusk of a December evening.

[22] Andrew Tyrie, 'Subsidiarity—What Should the Government Do?', Institute of Economic Affairs, December 1990

Listening to him was an education. The Basque Country is in many ways similar to Wales. It is a mountainous country of comparable size with a slightly smaller population of just over two million people. The economy was built on coal-mining and steel-making, both of which largely disappeared at the same time as our own. There is continuing high unemployment, especially amongst the young.

The Basque language, after being suppressed during the Franco era, is at present undergoing a revival led by Basque-medium schools and the Basque television channel, *Euskal Telebista* whose audience share is similar to that of *S4C*. Euskera is spoken by about 25 per cent of the population and the proportion is rising.

Senor Garro told us how they had dealt with the coal and steel run-down during the 1980s. 'We could not shield the country from the recessiion,' he said. 'But we could soften the blows, and with strategic planning make determined efforts to plan and diversify the economy which are now beginning to pay off.'

In particular, with its total control of taxes (a proportion of which the Basque Government hands over to Madrid) the government offered tax-breaks to specific firms in carefully chosen locations aimed at creating clusters of compatible industries. It promoted a consensus between employers' and workers' organizations, set in motion a training programme geared to high technology, and began a network of motorways that now link to the main European arteries.

Senor Garro sees the Basque Country's future as bound up with integration inside the European Community. Power, he said, will gradually accumulate to Brussels and at the same time to the smaller European nations and regions. 'In this process the biggest problem will be defining the role of the nation-states and in our case Spain. The problem is what to do about Madrid. But we should be able to agree a division of authority between all these levels, while keeping a respect for democracy, liberty and solidarity between nations. At the same time we should observe the principle of what we call subsidiarity, that is powers and functions should always be carried out at the lowest possible level of government. That is what Basque nationalism is about today.'

This interview took place in 1989 and was the first time I heard the word 'subsidiarity'. A little over a year later I was travelling in Baden Wurttemberg, one of the more prosperous Lander states in southern Germany, and called to see Erhard Eppler. Now retired, he has long been one of the foremost of the German SPD politicians, occupying ministerial positions in the Bonn central government, but also for many years leading the SPD opposition in the Baden-Wurttemberg Landtag Parliament in Stuttgart.

He spoke about the economic advantages Germany's federal system, established by the Allies after World War II, had brought. It had resulted in strong regional banks that made investing in the regional economy a priority. In Baden Wurttemberg the regional government had created a sophisticated range of institutions, connected with higher education, concerned with technology research and development, building on an already powerful engineering industrial base.

I asked Erhard Eppler two questions. Was there such a thing as competing identities in Germany, such as those we had in the United Kingdom, where a person might feel both Welsh and British? 'Oh yes,' he replied. 'Take myself, for instance. I am Swabian first and a German second.'

What did he feel had been achieved during his long years as leader of the Opposition in the Landtag Parliament? 'Well, we managed to stop a lot of things,' he answered with a wry smile. 'In particular a motorway they wanted to build across the Black Forest. But that's what democracy is all about.'

The message for Wales in these experiences is clear, and the linking motivation is democracy. By now there is a consensus on the need for an elected Welsh Assembly amongst the Welsh Labour Party, the Welsh Liberal Democrats and Plaid Cymru. Between them they won more than 70 per cent of the Welsh vote in the 1992 General Election.

The obstacle, of course, remains the Conservatives who sometimes give the impression that they believe democracy begins and ends at Westminster, whether the additional claims be those of the European Parliament or local and Welsh national government. Yet their record in Wales presents something of a paradox. On the one hand their control of the Welsh Office over more than a decade has promoted the administrative identity of Wales, giving us a markedly different profile from that which has applied in England. On the other hand, the Conservative objective has also been to integrate Wales more fully into mainstream British life, in both economic and cultural terms.

Economically they have succeeded, certainly to the extent that the M4 corridor has dragged much of coastal south Wales into the orbit of southern England.

Whether Welsh cultural values are heading in the same direction, however, is more questionable. Politically at any rate, the Conservatives in Wales have made relatively little progress. Despite the economic upheavals and modernization of the past twenty years, their vote has remained remarkably stable, between 25 and 30 per cent. As ever the number of Conservative Parliamentary seats has continued to depend on a lottery determined by the first-past-the-post electoral system combined with the variable fortunes of the other parties.

Nonetheless, the Conservatives continue to rule Wales, albeit as a minority Welsh party, using the strength of their overwhelming vote in southern England. It is a position that presents the Opposition parties in Wales with a democratic challenge. If they can work together to produce an agreed formula for improving Welsh democracy there is hope that events in the 1990s will provide an opening for change.

Any alternative political programme for reform must start from the reality of the Welsh Office bureaucratic state as it exists. It must seek to consolidate Welsh Office control over key remaining institutions in Wales—most notably, those in broadcasting. But much more fundamentally, it must seek to ensure democratic control of the Welsh Office itself through an elected Assembly with both financial and legislative autonomy. Only then will economic and cultural regeneration be pursued democratically, according to the wishes, and to the benefit, of the majority of the people of Wales.